MW01232673

SPANISH SHORT STORIES FOR BEGINNERS

Become Fluent in Less Than 30 Days
Using a Proven Scientific Method Applied in These Language Lessons.
Practice Vocabulary, Conversation & Grammar Daily
(series 3)

Table of Contents

INTRODUCTION

Welcome to "Spanish Short Stories for Beginners: How To Learn Latin American Accent Quickly with 50 Language Lessons in your Car for a Better Speaking, Listening and Conversation in Spanish Language (Part 1)". In this book, you will find a collection of short stories that will help you get a head start on learning Spanish in a quick and simple fashion.

Learning Spanish, like any other language, can be a challenging task. But it doesn't have to more challenging than it needs to. In fact, most books, methods and courses out there guarantee results in a short period of time. However, they don't take the time to present learners with the fundamentals that will enable them to make the most of their learning experience.

That is why this book is focused on providing you with the fundamentals that you will need in order to learn Spanish for the first time, or to brush up on your current skills. After all, why not make the most of your time and effort by learning another language?

As a matter of fact, being able to speak a foreign language, not to mention multiple languages, is a skill which is always in demand. While you may not actually get a job based on your linguistic competence alone, your ability to speak other languages will set you apart from anyone else in the business world.

What is you are keen on learning Spanish because you would like to travel? Then we've got you covered, too. You can take these lessons as a means of getting a grasp on the fundamentals that you will need in order to navigate your way through Spanish-speaking countries. If you are learning Spanish because you are looking to take on a new challenge, then by all means, go right ahead and take advantage of this opportunity to do so.

The fact of the matter is that learning Spanish doesn't have to an overwhelming task. With the tips, techniques and strategies that we will outline in this book, you will have a very good sense of how you can go about using the lessons contained herein to improve your Spanish skills.

Furthermore, you will be able to learn how to learn any language as the tips, techniques and strategies can be applied to virtually any language out there.

So, what are you waiting for?

The longer you wait to take on this challenge, the longer it will take you to achieve your goal of speaking another language. Whether Spanish is your second language, or your third, fourth, fifth, and so on, you will find the content in this book easy to manage.

As such, you won't have to work harder than you have to. You will have the right tools to achieve your goals in the shortest amount of time possible.

Please bear in mind that there is one essential ingredient in learning Spanish, or any language for that matter: consistency. Please make the effort to be consistent in your endeavors to learn this wonderful language. You will find that consistency will make things a lot easier for you.

See you on the inside.

SECTION I

FUNDAMENTALS OF LEARNING SPANISH

Tips and Strategies for Learning Spanish

In this chapter, we will be taking a look at useful tips, techniques and strategies which you can use to learn Spanish. As a matter of fact, the information contained in this chapter can be easily extrapolated to the learning of any language and not just Spanish. As such, you can feel confident that the content in this chapter is applicable well beyond this book.

For most folks, learning a language can seem like a daunting task. The main reason behind this lies in the fact that most folks are unfamiliar with the dynamic of learning a language. Consequently, they don't really know where to begin and how to make the most of their efforts.

Hence, many language learners tend to quit after a while because they can't seem to gain enough traction. This leads to frustration as struggling with a new language is never a pleasant experience. However, much of the frustration and struggles can be avoided by learning the ropes of how languages work.

The underpinnings of any language lie in the way the language is structured. In the case of Spanish, its basis lies in the conjugation of verbs. This means that you must become familiar with the various verb conjugations in order to fully understand how to structure the various verb tenses used throughout the language.

This can be a bit complicated with Romance languages. So, French, Spanish, Italian, Portuguese and Romanian receive the denomination of "Romance" languages since they are mainly derived from Latin which was the language of the old Roman Empire.

Over the centuries, each one of these languages has acquired its own nuances that make it unique. While they all have the same underpinnings, the visible surface can be quite different. Thus, it is important to get a firm understanding of how these languages work.

In this book, we will predominantly focus on the present tense as it is the most widely used tense in the Spanish language. Most Spanish speakers tend to use what are known as "simple" tenses since they tend to focus on just one tense at a time.

This is a stark contrast to the English language as most English speakers are able to weave their way in and out of various verb tenses. This can make conversation rather complex especially when topics warrant the use of several verb tenses.

The starting point with the Spanish language lies with the infinitive form of verbs. Verbs that do not have a verb tense are known as "infinitives". In other words, this is their pure form prior to being conjugated into a specific verb tense. In English, the infinitive form of verbs is written out as "to play" for example.

In Spanish, the infinitive form of verbs is defined by the ending of each verb. As such, there are three main forms in which infinitive verbs end. This is what will become the basis of the conjugation for each verb.

The other factor that will determine the manner in which a verb must be conjugated is the subject of the sentence. This is exactly the same as English. As such, depending on the subject that agrees with the verb, the verb must be conjugated in a specific manner.

So, let's take a look at the subject pronouns which can be used in Spanish.

- Yo (I)
- Tú (you, singular)
- Él (he)
- Ella (she)
- Nosotros (we)
- Ellos (they, masculine)
- Ellas (they, feminine)
- Ustedes (you, plural)

SPANISH SHORT STORIES FOR BEGINNERS

This list above presents the subject pronouns which are used in the Spanish language. Thus, this opens the door for a couple of important aspects to consider.

First, you will notice that there is a singular and a plural "you". In English, "you" is used to refer to both singular and plural nouns. So, "you are a teacher" and "you are teachers" use the same subject pronoun though its function is different.

Please note that English is an outlier in this regard as virtually all languages make a distinction between the singular and plural versions of "you". As such, it is important to keep this mind as you navigate throughout the texts and conversation you find in Spanish.

You may also encounter "vosotros" as another plural version of "you". This form tends to be considered archaic in Latin America and is not used outside of Spain. You may hear Spaniards use this form, but you will almost never hear it used in Latin America.

Another important distinction between English and most other languages, especially Romance languages, is the use of the masculine and feminine for nouns. English is a gender-neutral language. What this means is that nouns do not receive a "male" or "female" denomination. Nouns are simply referred to in a single, genderless tone.

Spanish assigns a gender to all nouns. This might get a bit tricky as determining which nouns are masculine and which nouns are feminine can be tough. But rest assured that with practice and experience, you will be able to get a firm grasp on this. We will be taking a deeper look at this in the next chapter.

One other fundamental difference between Romance languages and English is the various ways in which you can address a person. In Spanish, there are two main forms in which you can address a person. The most common form is "tú". This form is an informal "you". It can be used to address people of a similar age, station or friends, family and other acquaintances with whom you have a high degree of familiarity.

In the case of "usted", this is the formal version of "you". This form is used to refer to people who are much older than you, have a higher station, such as an employer, or people with whom you are not very familiar, for example, new acquaintances whom you've just met.

With these fundamentals in mind, let's take a look at learning strategies which you can use throughout this book.

Consistency is the biggest success factor you will encounter when learning a language. Regardless of whether you can devote 15 minutes, or 2 hours a day, the most important thing to keep in mind is that a consistent amount of time dedicated to learning will go a long way.

In this regard, most folks "binge learn", that is, they will not touch their books for days and then spend hours on end trying to make up the time. Think about it along these lines: imagine you do not go to the gym for a week and then you decide to spend 3 hours working out on a Saturday morning. What do you think the result of that would be?

The same principle applies to language learning.

- Repetition is another success factor. When you go over your lessons multiple times, you will be able to better fixate information and knowledge into your mind. After all, humans are not built to learn things instantaneously. Humans need practice and repetition before they can master any skill. That same concept applies to language. The more practice you get, the more your skills will improve.

- Keep a learning diary. Keeping a learning diary, or a log of your activities, will help you visualize what you are doing to help yourself learn. In other words, you are keeping track of your language learning tasks. What this does is help you to see what works and doesn't. Later on, you can always refer back to those tasks which are providing you with the most value and which ones are not.

- Making handwritten notes will help fixate knowledge much better. Of course, using your phone, laptop or tablet makes life a lot easier. However, making handwritten notes enables the brain to involve more senses in the learning process. As such, individual words and grammar will permeate your mind in such a way that the mechanics of grammar, word order and spelling become clear in your mind.

- Use a tool such as www.spanishdict.com as a grammar and conjugation reference. In addition, this tool will also provide you with the pronunciation of words. Consequently, you will have a tool that can support you when you are working on your own. Furthermore, it is a great study tool or just serve as a reference when you are curious about something related to your Spanish lessons.

Now, let's look at a suggested methodology which you can use to help you get the most out of this book. Of course, this is not the only way that you can take advantage of the material in this book. Nevertheless, this methodology is designed to help you utilize the contents of this book to the fullest.

1. Firstly, read each story once, all the way through. At first, it will be hard to make sense of its contents. However, as you go through the story, you will see some words which resemble English words. These words, most of the time, will basically be the same English word. For example, "responsable" and "responsible" resemble each other almost identically. And yes, they have the same meaning. Consider this: "police" and "policía". It is practically the same word. So, you can highlight, or underline, these words and make note of them.

2. Next, go through the text a second time. You will see your comprehension improving significantly. You will notice how similar-looking and sounding words make the text a lot easier to understand.

3. After, go through the text highlighting, or underlining, words which are completely unfamiliar to you. Hopefully there won't be that many, but there will be

some of these words. This will help you to visualize how much of the vocabulary is actually new to you.

4. Then, you can use a tool such as www.spanishdict.com or www.wordreference.com to help you find the meaning, pronunciation and usage of these new vocabulary items.

5. Once you have found translations, synonyms and equivalent meanings, you can then proceed to run through the entire text one more time. You will find that the text is now much more comprehensible that it once was. This will enable you to make greater sense of the content in each lesson.

6. After you feel comfortable with the language in the lesson, you can proceed to the questions located at the end of the lesson. The questions are intended to help you gain further practice into question formation, word order and reading comprehension. The questions have been designed to be open-ended. As such, there is no single way of answering. Nevertheless, we have taken care to provide suggested responses in order to provide you with guidance.

7. Once you feel confident in answering each question, you go back and give the text one more run through. You can read the text aloud for further practice. If you are shy about your pronunciation, pick a time when you are alone and go through it.

8. If you so choose, you can use a tool such as the Text to Speech plugin for Google Chrome to read the text for you. This will give you a great sense of how the text is pronounced. As such, you will be able to get the perfect pronunciation and thereby help you get the right pronunciation as well.

9. One good tip is to have a vocabulary notebook. You can use your learning journal to write down all of the vocabulary words which you encounter on a daily basis. What this enables you to do is to keep track of all the new words that you learn on a given day. Thus, the act of writing things down by hand will help to further fixate ideas in your mind.

10. Lastly, watching Spanish language content on television or online will also help you to practice your listening skills while allowing you to learn more vocabulary and grammar. So, do try to make the most of the opportunities around to improve your Spanish skills.

With these tips and strategies, you will be well on your way to improving your overall Spanish skills. In the next chapter we will be taking a closer look at language aspects which tend to be particularly tricky for English speakers.

Common Problems when Learning Spanish

In this chapter, we are going to be looking at the various problem areas that English speakers generally tend to have when they seek out to learn Spanish. As such, we will be going over them in this chapter so as to provide insight and recommendations on how to deal with them as you progress through your Spanish learning endeavors.

Earlier, we established that Spanish, just like French and Italian, is a Romance language. In contrast, English is of Germanic origin. What this means is that English and Spanish were born in different neighborhoods. Nevertheless, they do have one, common thread: French.

The influence of French upon the English language has led it to have some striking similarities with Spanish. However, there are enough difference between both languages to throw a monkey wrench into anyone's learning endeavors.

What does this mean?

It means that when English speakers go about learning Spanish, they will run into some essential differences that will be challenging at first, but don't necessarily have to insurmountable. As such, it is important to understand these differences in order to make them more accessible to learners.

The first big difference is gender.

Gender tends to be one of the biggest sources of frustration to Spanish learners as there is no clear rule or guideline to determine which objects are masculine and which ones are feminine. The easiest way to identify gender among nouns is by observing the article that precedes it.

For example, "el" is used for masculine and "la" is used for feminine. So, "el sol" (the sun) is masculine whereas "la luna" is feminine. This is a good rule of thumb to follow when you are reading a text or simply hearing regular conversation.

However, it gets tricky when you see, or think, of an object but you are unaware of the article that precedes it. In this case, it can be tough to figure out the gender of an object. Since there really is no way to determine this just by looking at the object itself, there is one way in which you can figure this out: look at the object's name.

In general, the names of masculine nouns end in "o" and feminine nouns end in "a". This is a good rule of thumb to follow as the endings will help you to figure out their gender.

For instance, these are some examples of masculine nouns:

- Carro (car)
- Niño (boy)
- Palo (stick)
- Mono (monkey)
- Zapato (shoe)

As you can see, these nouns are all masculine given their endings. Also, there are some exceptions which you can keep an eye out for. Nouns that end in "ma" and "pa" are masculine. For example, "mapa" (map) and "problema" (problem) are masculine.

There are also some other exceptions such as:

- Papel
- Hombre
- Doctor
- Autobus
- Atún

These nouns don't have a regular "o/a" ending yet they are considered masculine.

Regarding feminine nouns, the general rule of thumb is that they end in an "a". Here are some examples:

- Cama (bed)
- Casa (house)
- Planta (plant)
- Mamá (mother)
- Hoja (leaf)

As you can see, these are feminine nouns based on the fact that they end in "a". However, there are some exceptions as always. Nouns that end in "ión" such as "relación" (relation), "dad/tad" such as "Amistad" (friendship) and "tud" such as "solictud" (request) are considered feminine.

Also, another good rule of thumb is that nouns can be converted into feminine by adding an "a" to it. For instance, "doctor" which is masculine, can become feminine as "doctora". Also, "enfermero" (nurse, male) would become "enfermera" (nurse, female) by simply substituting the "o" for the "a" ending.

Also, there are a couple of interesting exceptions:

- La mano (hand) is feminine despite ending in an "o".
- La radio (the radio) is feminine despite ending in an "o".
- La noche (night) is also feminine.

Please keep in mind that Spanish always uses the articles "el" and "la" to precede the reference to a noun. Conversely, English does not use this form unless the speaker is being specific about the noun in question.

With this guide, you can begin to navigate your way through the world of masculine and feminine nouns. As you gain more practice and experience, you will find that it is actually rather straightforward. So, do take the time to go over them.

Another area to take into consideration is verb conjugation.

Unlike English, Spanish has a specific verb conjugation for verbs based on the subject that it agrees with and the verb tense.

This is rather simple and straightforward in the English language as verb conjugation does not necessarily imply radically modifying the verb's structure. However, Spanish does require verb endings to be changed in accordance to the subject it agrees with. But fear not, we will make this very straightforward.

The first thing to look out for is the ending of the verb in its infinitive form. As stated earlier, the infinitive form of a verb is when it has not been conjugated to agree with a subject in a particular verb tense. as such, the infinitive form of the verb is key in order to determine how it will be conjugated.

Verbs in the infinitive form in Spanish will end in one of three ways: "ar", "er" and "ir". So, let's take a look at some examples of this:

- Verbs ending in "ar"
- Estar (to be)
- Jugar (to play)
- Viajar (to travel)
- Cantar (to sing)
- Firmar (to sign)

Now, let's take a look at some verbs that end in "er":

- Verbs ending in "er":
- Comer (to eat)
- Volver (to return)
- Correr (to run)
- Resolver (to solve)
- Responder (to respond)

Here is a list of some verbs ending in "ir":

- Verbs ending in "ir"
- Abrir (to open)
- Cubrir (to cover)
- Sentir (to feel)
- Vivir (to live)
- Fingir (to fake)

The above examples are a small sample size of the verbs which you will encounter throughout your study of the Spanish language. As such, let's take a look at how these verbs are conjugated in the present simple tense.

Here is a chart which explains the various endings for each subject and according to the verb ending.

Subject pronoun	AR	ER	IR
Yo (I)	o	o	o
Tú (you, singular)	as	es	es
Él (he)	a	e	e
Ella (she)	a	e	e
Nosotros (we)	amos	emos	imos
Ellos (they, masculine)	an	en	en
Ellas (they, feminine)	an	en	en
Ustedes (you, plural)	an	en	en

Figure 1. Verb endings in the present simple tense.

The chart above show the endings that are to be attached depending on the subject that a verb will agree with.

Hence, let's take a look at some examples in order to make this point evident.

- Infinitive: cantar (to sing)
- Yo canto (I sing)
- Tú cantas (you sing, singular)
- Él canta (he sings)
- Ella canta (she sings)
- Nosotros cantamos (we sing)
- Ellos cantan (they sing, masculine)
- Ellas cantan (they sing, feminine)
- Ustedes cantan (you sing, plural)

As you can see, the original "ar" ending is dropped in favor of the corresponding ending based on the subject. With the exception of a handful of irregular verbs, this is the rule of thumb to follow with verbs ending in "ar".

Consequently, the same pattern applies to the verbs ending in "er" and "ir". Let's have a look at some examples.

- Infinitive: vivir (to live)
- Yo vivo (I live)
- Tú vives (you live, singular)
- Él vive (he lives)
- Ella vive (she lives)
- Nosotros vivimos (we live)
- Ellos viven (they live, masculine)
- Ellas viven (they live, feminine)
- Ustedes viven (you live, plural)

As with the "ar" verbs, the "ir" ending is dropped in favor of the corresponding ending. Let's take a look at an example of an "er" verb.

- Infinitive: comer (to eat)
- Yo como (I eat)
- Tú comes (you eat, singular)
- Él come (he eats)
- Ella come (she eats)
- Nosotros comemos (we eat)
- Ellos comen (they eat, masculine)

- Ellas comen (they eat, feminine)
- Ustedes comen (you eat, plural)

Given the previous examples, the conjugation of verbs in the present simple are rather straightforward. Of course, it takes some time and practice. Nevertheless, you can become proficient with verb conjugations in a relatively short period of time. As such, all you need is to dedicate some time and effort in to practicing the way verbs are to be conjugated. If you are ever in doubt, www.spanishdict.com is a great tool which you can consult in order to get the right conjugation.

Another significant difference between English and Spanish is the use of subjects, or lack thereof, in sentences. In Spanish it is quite common to omit the use of a subject at the beginning of sentence especially when it is clear who is being referred to in the conversation. As such, speakers will often take the liberty of omitting the subject observing only the proper conjugation of the verb.

Needless to say, this can cause confusion even among native Spanish speakers. The reason for this is that unless there is a clear understanding of who is being referred to, it can be very difficult to keep track of a conversation.

Let's look at an example:

- Soy de los Estados Unidos (I am from the United States).

In this example, the use of the from "soy" (am) is the proper conjugation for the verb "ser" (to be) in the present simple tense. However, it is rather clear that "soy" refers to "I am", hence, a Spanish speaker would be more than willing to dump "yo" (I) give the fact that it is perfectly clear that this individual is referring to themselves.

So, do keep an eye out for this type of omission as you will frequently see it throughout the text presented in this book.

On the subject of the verb "ser", the Spanish language has two versions of the verb "to be". One is "ser" and the other is "estar". As such, let's take a look at their difference and their conjugation. In essence, the difference in "ser" and "estar" lies in the fact that "ser" refers to permanent, or often unchangeable attributes, whereas "estar" refers to temporary or changeable characteristics.

For example, when referring to your occupation, you can say "soy abogado" (I am a lawyer). This makes it clear that your occupation is permanent and won't be changing any time soon. On the other hand, you can say "estoy feliz" (I am happy). This is a totally changeable proposition as your mood is far more changeable than your occupation.

The distinction between both forms of "to be" in Spanish are very useful when you are talking about yourself, or perhaps you are talking about the way you feel and the location of people and things. Consequently, the conjugation of each verb is also different.

Let's look at the conjugation of "ser":

- Infinitive: ser (to be)
- Yo soy (I am)
- Tú eres (you are, singular)
- Él es (he is)
- Ella es (she is)
- Nosotros somos (we are)
- Ellos son (they are, masculine)
- Ellas son (they are, feminine)
- Ustedes son (you are, plural)

Please note that "ser" is irregular as the base form of the verb changes in order to accommodate its corresponding ending as an "er" verb.

Here is the conjugation for the "estar" version of "to be":

- Infinitive: estar (to be)
- Yo estoy (I am)
- Tú estás (you are, singular)
- Él está (he is)
- Ella está (she is)
- Nosotros estamos (we are)
- Ellos están (they are, masculine)
- Ellas están (they are, feminine)
- Ustedes están (you are, plural)

Once again, "estar" is an irregular verb. This version of "to be" differs greatly from the usual verb endings for "ar" verbs even though its base does not change significantly.

In addition, please bear in mind that "estar" is the verb which is used with the present continuous. It serves as the auxiliary verb which provides the tense to the "ando" and "iendo" endings of the verbs that must be conjugated in order to make the present continuous.

Now, the present continuous is used in exactly the same fashion as it is in English; the present continuous is used to indicate when there is a temporary action either happening at the time of speaking or around the time of speaking. Thus, the most important element to consider is that the present continuous is a temporary action whereas the present simple is used to indicate more permanent actions.

Let's take a look at an example:

- Estoy practicando español (I am practicing Spanish).

In this example, you are indicting an action that is happening at the time of speaking, that is, you are practicing Spanish at this very moment. Also, it can refer to an action which is happening around the present. For instance, you could be practicing your Spanish with other individuals though you are not practicing Spanish right at the moment of speaking.

The present continuous is constructed with the "estar" version of to be. Furthermore, the main verb is then modified to include the "ando" or "iendo" ending.

Let's take a look at how that works.

- "ar" verbs end in "ando"
- "er" verbs end in "iendo"
- "ir" verbs end in "iendo".

Here are some examples:

- Nosotros estamos jugando fútbol. (We are playing soccer)
- Ustedes están comiendo carne. (You are eating meat)
- Ella está viviendo en Buenos Aires. (She is living in Buenos Aires)

Please notice how the main conjugation happens with the verb "estar" while the main verb is conjugated to the "ando" and "endo" form. It should be noted that this ending is not specific to the subject. The agreement with the subject occurs with "estar". Therefore, the main verb does need to be transformed to suit the individual subject in question. This makes it far easier to get a grasp on this tense as you won't have to conjugate each verb based on individual subjects.

With this, we have laid the groundwork for the content in this book. We are now ready to move on to the short stories prepared for your study. Please keep in mind that nothing is ever cast in stone when it comes to language. Nevertheless, the patterns which we have laid out herein will provide you with a good head start when it comes to improving your Spanish skills.

The main thing to keep in mind is that consistency will give you the best chance to improve your skills regardless of your starting point. Hence, if you can devote a certain amount of time, on a regular basis, the likelihood of your Spanish skills improving will increase significantly.

So, please sit back and enjoy the short stories that have been prepared for you. They are designed to be both educational and entertaining. Please remember to go over them as many times as you need so that you can get the most out of the contents and materials presented in this book.

Let's move on to the next section in this book.

SECTION II

THE VERB "SER" AND "ESTAR"

Lesson 1:
Present Simple with verb "estar"

Español	English
De viaje por Europa	**Traveling in Europe**
Vocabulario importante:	**Important vocabulary:**
agradable	pleasant
clima	weather

después	after
encerrada	locked up
moda	fashion
nubes	clouds
optimista	optimistic
oscuro	dark
piscina	pool
triste	sad

Estoy de viaje por Europa. En este momento, estoy en Francia. Es un país bello con muchos lugares preciosos. El clima en París durante el verano es muy **agradable**. La temperatura es cálida, el cielo es azul, y las flores son hermosas.

I'm traveling in Europe. At this moment, I am in France. It is a beautiful country with many beautiful places. The weather in Paris during the summer is very **pleasant**. The temperature is warm, the sky is blue, and the flowers are beautiful.

Pero hoy el clima está horrible. El cielo está **oscuro**. El viento está muy fuerte. La temperatura está baja. Esto no es un día de verano. Es mi mala suerte hoy. Estoy **encerrada** en mi hotel. Estoy muy preocupada por la lluvia. Las **nubes** están listas para la lluvia.

But today the weather is horrible. The sky is **dark**. The wind is very strong. The temperature is low. This is not a summer day. It's my bad luck today. I'm **locked up** in my hotel. I'm very worried about the rain. The **clouds** are ready for the rain.

Estoy en mi habitación ahora. Pero, mis hermanas están en la **piscina** del hotel. Ellas están felices a pesar del **clima**. Es cierto, la piscina del hotel es está

I'm in my room now. But, my sisters are in the hotel **pool**. They are happy despite the **weather**. It's true, the hotel's

grande y divertida. Pero los sitios alrededor de París también están impresionantes. Estoy ilusionada con los Campos Elisios. Es un lugar impresionante. Por eso estoy tan **triste** en este momento.

Mi padre está convencido la lluvia está lejos. Él está seguro de la posibilidad un buen clima para esta tarde. Estoy optimista de eso. Una buena tarde es todo lo que necesito para estar feliz en París. Todo está perfecto menos el clima de esta mañana. La comida es perfecta. La **moda** es alucinante. Las tiendas son fabulosas… ¡pero el clima no!

Mi madre está en la habitación conmigo. Ella también está convencida del buen clima para esta tarde. Ella es tan **optimista** como yo. Las dos estamos seguras de una buena tarde por las calles de París. Es una ciudad tan bella. Por eso estoy triste por el clima terrible hoy.

Pero, el hotel está muy bonito, ¡eso sí! Este hotel es fabuloso. Quizá mi día no está tan mal **después** de todo. Estoy en una habitación muy cómoda. Estoy bien con mi familia por el momento.

pool is big and fun. But the sites around Paris are also impressive. I'm excited about the Champs Elysees. It is an awesome place. That's why I'm so **sad** at the moment.

My father is convinced the rain is far away. He is sure of the possibility a good weather for this afternoon. I'm optimistic about that. A good afternoon is all I need to be happy in Paris. Everything is perfect except this morning's weather. The food is perfect. **Fashion** is amazing. The shops are fabulous ... but the weather is not!

My mother is in the room with me. She is also convinced of the good weather for this afternoon. She is as **optimistic** as I am. We are both sure of a good afternoon on the streets of Paris. It is such a beautiful city. That's why I'm sad because of the terrible weather today.

But, the hotel is very nice, yes! This hotel is fabulous. Maybe my day is not so bad **after** all.

I'm in a very comfortable room. I'm fine with my family at the moment.

Por favor responda las siguientes preguntas.

Please answer the following questions.

¿Por dónde estoy de viaje?

Where am I on holiday?

_____

____

_____

____

_____

____

¿Cómo es el clima de París en verano?

What is the weather like in Paris in the summer?

_____

____

_____

____

_____

____

¿Cómo está el clima hoy?

What is the weather like today?

_____

____

_____

____

_____

____

_____
____

¿Para qué están listas las nubes?

_____
____

_____
____

_____
____

¿Dónde están mis hermanas?

_____
____

_____
____

_____
____

_____
____

¿Qué es lo que necesito para estar feliz?

_____
____

_____
____

_____
____

_____
What are the clouds ready for?

_____
____

_____
____

_____
____

Where are my sisters?

_____
____

_____
____

_____
____

_____
____

What do I need to be happy?

_____
____

_____
____

_____
____

_____

___

¿Cómo es el hotel?   What is the hotel like?

_____   _____

___   ___

_____   _____

___   ___

_____   _____

___   ___

¿De qué está convencido mi   What is my father convinced
padre?   about?

_____   _____

___   ___

_____   _____

___   ___

_____   _____

___   ___

¿Cómo es mi madre?   What is my mother like?

_____   _____

___   ___

_____   _____

___   ___

_____

_____

_____

¿Cómo es París?   What is Paris like?

_____

_____

_____

_____

_____

_____

_____

_____

Respuestas sugeridas	Suggested answers
¿Por dónde estoy de viaje?	Where am I on holiday?
<u>Estoy de viaje por Europa.</u>	<u>I am in Europe on holiday</u>
¿Cómo es el clima de París en verano?	What is the weather like in Paris in the summer?
<u>El clima en París en verano es muy agradable.</u>	<u>The weather is very pleasant in Paris in the summer.</u>
¿Cómo está el clima hoy?	What is the weather like today?
<u>El clima está horrible hoy.</u>	<u>The weather is horrible today.</u>
¿Para qué están listas las nubes?	What are the clouds ready for?
<u>Las nubes están listas para la lluvia.</u>	<u>The clouds are ready for rain,</u>
¿Dónde están mis hermanas?	Where are my sisters?
<u>Mis hermanas están en la piscina del hotel.</u>	<u>They are in the hotel pool.</u>
¿Qué es lo que necesito para estar feliz?	What do I need to be happy?
<u>Una buena tarde es todo lo que</u>	<u>I need a good afternoon to be happy.</u>

necesito para ser feliz.

¿Cómo es el hotel?	What is the hotel like?
El hotel es muy bonito y fabuloso.	The hotel is very nice and fabulous.
¿De qué está convencido mi padre?	What is my father convinced about?
Mi padre está convencido de que la lluvia está lejos.	My father is convinced that the ran is far away.
¿Cómo es mi madre?	What is my mother like?
Mi madre es tan optimista como yo.	My mother is as optimistic as I am.
¿Cómo es París?	What is Paris like?
París es una ciudad tan bella.	Paris is such a beautiful city.

Lesson 2:
Present Simple with verb "estar"

Español	English
Hora del almuerzo	**Lunch Time**

Vocabulario importante:	**Important vocabulary:**
almuerzo	lunch
complacido	pleased
hambrientas	hungry
hoy	today
humor	mood
jefe	boss
mediodía	midday
molesto	upset
reunión	meeting
sabroso	tasty

Son las 12:30 del **mediodía**. Ya es hora del almuerzo. Todas las personas en mi oficina están listas para la hora de la comida. Los elevadores están llenos de personas **hambrientas**. La cafetería de mi oficina también está llena de personas. Yo estoy en mi escritorio. Estoy atrasado con mi trabajo. Mi reporte está pendiente para hoy. Es un trabajo largo. Estoy hambriento pero mi trabajo es más

It's 12:30, at midday. It's time for lunch. All the people in my office are ready for lunch. The elevators are full of hungry people. The cafeteria in my office is also full of people. I am at my desk. I'm late with my work. My report is pending for today. It is a long work. I'm hungry but my work is more important.

34

importante.

Hoy, mi **almuerzo** es un sándwich de jamón y queso con un refresco de bebida. Sí, es cierto, los refrescos no son saludables. Pero por hoy, está bien. **Hoy** no es un día fácil. Por eso, está bien un refresco... pero sólo uno. También es día para mucho café.

Today, my lunch is a ham and cheese sandwich with a soft drink. Yes, it's true, soft drinks are not healthy. But for today, it's fine. Today is not an easy day. That's why a soda is fine ... but only one. It is also a day for a lot of coffee.

Soy contador en una empresa muy grande en Boston. Mi **jefe** es una muy buena persona, pero es muy exigente. Hoy, está de mal humor. No es un buen día. Por eso está sumamente **molesto**. Está enojado por los resultados de la empresa. Por eso mi reporte es tan importante para la reunión de esta tarde. Está casi listo, pero mis compañeros y yo estamos contra el tiempo. Ellos están preocupados al igual que yo.

I'm an accountant in a very large company in Boston. My boss is a very good person, but he is very demanding. Today, he is in a bad mood. It's not a good day. That's why he is extremely upset. He is angry about the results of the company. That's why my report is so important for this afternoon's meeting. It's almost ready, but my teammates and I are running out of time. They are worried just like me.

El trabajo está complicado, pero no imposible. Es cierto, estamos cansados, pero estamos listos para la gran **reunión** de esta tarde. Estamos seguros de que nuestro jefe está optimista a pesar de estar de mal humor. Él siempre está listo para las reuniones importantes.

The work is complicated, but not impossible. It's true, we're tired, but we're ready for this big meeting this afternoon. We are sure that our boss is optimistic despite being in a bad mood. He is always ready for important

Mi sándwich de jamón y queso está delicioso. El refresco también está **sabroso**. Es el almuerzo de un día complicado. Es un día con mucho trabajo, pero también de mucha satisfacción.

¡Mi reporte está listo! Está listo justo a tiempo para la reunión de esta tarde. Estoy **complacido** con mi esfuerzo. Mis compañeros y yo estamos satisfechos por el buen trabajo de hoy.

meetings.

My ham and cheese sandwich is delicious. The soda is also tasty. It's a lunch for a complicated day. It is a day with a lot of work, but also a lot of satisfaction.

My report is ready! It's ready just in time for this afternoon's meeting. I am pleased with my effort. My colleagues and I are satisfied with today's good work.

Por favor responda las siguientes preguntas.

Please answer the following questions.

¿Para qué están listas las personas en mi oficina?

What are the people in my office ready for?

_____
___
_____
___
_____
___

¿Para cuándo está pendiente el reporte?

When is the report pending?

_____
___
_____
___
_____
___
_____
___

¿Cuál es mi trabajo?

What is my job?

_____
___
_____
___
_____

———

_____

———

¿Para cuándo es el reporte?   When is the report due?

_____   _____

———   ———

_____   _____

———   ———

_____   _____

———   ———

¿Cuál es mi almuerzo?   What is my lunch?

_____   _____

———   ———

_____   _____

———   ———

_____   _____

———   ———

¿Cómo es nuestro jefe?   What is our boss like?

_____   _____

———   ———

_____   _____

———   ———

¿Cómo está el refresco?

What is the soda like?

¿Cómo es el día de hoy?

What is today like?

¿Cómo estoy por mi trabajo?

How am I feeling because of my work?

———

————————————————

———

¿Cómo están mis compañeros por su trabajo?

————————————————

———

————————————————

———

————————————————

———

————————————————————

———

————————————————————

———

How are my colleagues feeling because of their work?

————————————————————

———

————————————————————

———

————————————————————

———

Respuestas sugeridas	Suggested answers
¿Para qué están listas las personas en mi oficina?	What are the people in my office ready for?
Las personas en mi oficina están listas para el almuerzo.	The people in my office are ready for lunch.
¿Para cuándo está pendiente el reporte?	When is the report pending?
El reporte está pendiente para hoy.	The report is pending for today.
¿Cuál es mi trabajo?	What is my job?
Soy contador en una empresa.	I am an accountant in a company.
¿Para cuándo es el reporte?	When is the report for?
El reporte es para hoy.	The report is for today.
¿Cuál es mi almuerzo?	What is my lunch?
Mi almuerzo es un sándwich de jamón y queso.	My lunch is a ham and cheese sandwich.

¿Cómo es nuestro jefe?	What is our boss like?
Nuestro jefe es muy bueno persona, pero es muy exigente.	Our boss is a very nice person, but he is very demanding.
¿Cómo está el refresco?	What is the soda like?
El refresco está sabroso	The soda is very tasty.
¿Cómo es el día de hoy?	What is today like?
Hoy es un día complicado.	Today is a complicated day.
¿Cómo estoy por mi trabajo?	How am I feeling because of my work?
Estoy complacido con mi esfuerzo.	I am pleased with my effort.
¿Cómo están mis compañeros por su trabajo?	How are my colleagues feeling because of their work?
Mis compañeros están satisfechos por el buen trabajo de hoy.	My colleagues are satisfied with today's work.

SECTION III

THE PRESENT SIMPLE TENSE

Lesson 3:
Present Simple with "ER" verbs

Español	English
El clima de mi ciudad	The Weather in my City
Vocabulario importante:	Important vocabulary:
aburrido	boring
año	year
complace	pleases
divertidas	fun

durante	during
estación	season
fríos	cold
lluviosos	rainy
nublados	cloudy
soleados	sunny

El clima de mi ciudad es muy variado. Según la **estación** del año, el clima puede ser cálido o frío. No siempre es igual. Hay días en que el clima es muy cálido y otros días en que llueve mucho. Los días **lluviosos** no son divertidos porque no puedo hacer mis actividades favoritas. Hago mis tareas en casa y veo televisión.

En los días **soleados**, puedo hacer muchas cosas. Hago deportes como la natación y el fútbol, corro en el parque, veo el paisaje o leo al aire libre. Esa es una de mis actividades favoritas. Leer me **complace** mucho. Puedo leer horas y horas cuando estoy al aire libre. Creo que todos estamos felices cuando hace buen tiempo.

En mi ciudad hay días soleados, **nublados**, **fríos**, cálidos, y lluviosos. Los días soleados son

The weather of my city is quite varied. Depending on the **season**, the weather can be hot or cold. It is not always the same. There are days when the weather is very hot and other days when it rains a lot. **Rainy** days are not fun because I cannot do my favorite activities. I do my homework and I watch television.

On **sunny** days, I can do many things. I do sports like swimming and soccer, I run in the park, I see the landscape, or I read outdoors. That is one of my favorite activities. Reading pleases me a lot. I can read for hours and hours when I am outdoors. I think we're all happy when the weather is fine.

In my city there are sunny days, **cloudy**, **cold**, warm, and rainy. Sunny days are my favorite days.

mis días favoritos. En estos días prendemos la barbacoa y hacemos una comida deliciosa. También podemos estar en la piscina bajo el sol cálido. En definitiva, podemos hacer muchas cosas **divertidas** cuando el día está soleado.

These days we light the barbecue and make a delicious meal. We can also be in the pool under the warm sun. In short, we can do many **fun** things when the day is sunny.

Por el contrario, no podemos hacer mucho durante los días lluviosos. Lo único que podemos hacer es estar en casa. Tenemos la televisión, video juegos e internet, pero es **aburrido** después de muchas horas sin hacer algo fuera de casa. Pero, en los días lluviosos hacemos algo interesante: volvemos al pasado. Conocemos muchas historias de nuestra familia. Sabemos muchas cosas divertidas sobre nuestra comunidad.

On the contrary, we cannot do much during rainy days. The only thing we can do is be at home. We have television, video games and the internet, but it is boring after many hours without doing something outside the house. But, on rainy days we do something interesting: we go back to the past. We know many stories about our family. We know many fun things about our community.

Puedo hacer muchas cosas durante los días soleados. Esos son los mejores días del **año**. Pero también hay muchas cosas que puedo hacer **durante** los días lluviosos. Aunque no puedo estar afuera, es bonito estar en casa con mi familia. Podemos estar muchas horas juntos en la sala de nuestra casa. Creo que eso es lo mejor de los días lluviosos.

I can do many things during sunny days. These are the best days of the **year**. But there are also many things that I can do **during** the rainy days. Even though I cannot be outside, it's nice to be at home with my family. We can spend many hours together in the living room of our house. I think that's the best part the of rainy days.

LEARNING SPANISH ACADEMY

Por favor responda las siguientes preguntas.

Please answer the following questions.

¿Cómo es el clima de mi ciudad?

What is the weather like in my city?

_____
___
_____
___
_____
___
_____
___

_____
___
_____
___
_____
___

¿Por qué no son divertidos los días lluviosos?

Why are rainy days not fun?

_____
___
_____
___
_____
___
_____
___

_____
___
_____
___
_____
___

¿Qué hago en los días soleados?

What do I do on sunny days?

_____
___
_____
___
_____

_____
___
_____
___
_____

47

———

_____

———

¿Cuánto tiempo puedo leer al aire libre?

_____

———

_____

———

_____

———

¿Cómo son los días en mi ciudad?

_____

———

_____

———

_____

———

_____

———

¿Qué hacemos en los días soleados?

_____

———

———

_____

———

How long can I read outside?

_____

———

_____

———

_____

———

What are the days like in my city?

_____

———

_____

———

_____

———

_____

———

What do we do on sunny days?

_____

———

_____

_____

——

_____

——

_____

——

——

_____

——

_____

——

_____

——

¿Qué tenemos para los días lluviosos?

What do we have for rainy days?

_____

——

_____

——

_____

——

_____

——

_____

——

_____

——

_____

——

_____

——

¿Qué es interesante hacer durante los días lluviosos?

What is interesting to do on rainy days?

_____

——

_____

——

_____

——

_____

——

_____

——

_____

——

_____

——

¿Cuáles son los mejores días del

What are the best days of the

año?

year?

_____

_____

___

___

_____

_____

___

___

_____

_____

___

___

_____

_____

___

___

¿Qué es lo mejor de los días lluviosos?

What is the best part of rainy days?

_____

_____

___

___

_____

_____

___

___

_____

_____

___

___

_____

_____

___

___

Respuestas sugeridas	Suggested answers
¿Cómo es el clima de mi ciudad?	What is the weather like in my city?
El clima de mi ciudad es variado.	The weather in my city is quite varied.
¿Por qué no son divertidos los días lluviosos?	Why are rainy days not fun?
Porque no puedo hacer mis actividades favoritas.	Because I cannot do my favorite activities.
¿Qué hago en los días soleados?	What do I do on sunny days?
Hago deportes o leo al aire libre en los días soleados.	I do sports or read outside on sunny days.
¿Cuánto tiempo puedo leer al aire libre?	How long can I read outside?
Puedo leer por horas al aire libre.	I can read for hours outside.
¿Cómo son los días en mi ciudad?	What are the days like in my city?
En mi ciudad hay días nublados, fríos, cálidos, y lluviosos.	In my city, there are cloudy, cold, warm and rainy days.

¿Qué hacemos en los días soleados?	What do we do on sunny days?
<u>Prendemos la barbacoa o podemos estar en la piscina.</u>	<u>We fire up the barbecue or we can be in the pool.</u>
¿Qué tenemos para los días lluviosos?	What do we have for rainy days?
<u>Tenemos televisión, video juegos e internet.</u>	<u>We have television, video games and internet.</u>
¿Qué es interesante hacer durante los días lluviosos?	What is interesting to do on rainy days?
<u>Volver al pasado es divertido durante los días lluviosos.</u>	<u>We go back to the past during rainy days.</u>
¿Cuáles son los mejores días del año?	What are the best days of the year?
<u>Los días soleados son los mejores días del año.</u>	<u>Rainy days are the best days of the year.</u>
¿Qué es lo mejor de los días lluviosos?	What is the best part of rainy days?
<u>Estar juntos en la sala de nuestra casa es lo mejor de los días lluviosos.</u>	<u>Being together in the family room of our home is the best part of rainy days.</u>

Lesson 4:
Present Simple with "ER" verbs

Español	English
Ser exitoso	**Being Successful**

Vocabulario importante:	Important vocabulary:
acerca	about
aprender	learn
ascender	move up
contrato	contract
empleo	job
mañana	tomorrow
negocios	business
obtener	get
poquito	little bit
reglas	rules

Para ser exitoso en la vida, se debe **aprender** muchas cosas útiles e importantes. Cuando una persona aprende todo lo necesario para la vida, siempre tiene una buena oportunidad de tener éxito. Esta es una de las **reglas** esenciales de la vida.

To be successful in life, you must **learn** many useful and important things. When a person learns everything necessary for life, they always have a good chance of success. This is one of the essential **rules** of life.

Muchas personas piensan, "¿qué debo aprender?"

Many people think, "what should I learn?"

Hay muchas cosas por aprender. La vida está llena cosas que debemos conocer. Por ejemplo, debemos conocer **acerca** de la tecnología. Las computadoras y el internet son esenciales para el trabajo moderno. Si no sabes de tecnología, es difícil **obtener** un buen **empleo**. Las personas que saben mucho sobre tecnología obtienen buenos empleos en reconocidas empresas.

Para mí, ser exitoso depende de las cosas que sabes hacer bien. Si sabes hacer bien tu trabajo, siempre tienes oportunidades para **ascender** de puesto. Las empresas reconocen el trabajo de los buenos empleados mediante ascender de puesto o extender su **contrato**. Los buenos empleados siempre crecen en sus trabajos cuando ejercen una buena actitud. Por lo tanto, una buena actitud también es muy importante.

Mi gran esfuerzo es crecer cada día. Crezco cuando leo cosas interesantes, crezco cuando ejerzo mis habilidades y crezco cuando hago cosas útiles con mi tiempo. Si tú quieres crecer, debes hacer esto también. Si pierdes el tiempo en cosas que no son útiles, no creces. Para ser

There are many things to learn. Life is full of things we must know. For example, we should know **about** technology. Computers and the internet are essential for modern work. If you do not know about technology, it is difficult to **get** a good job. People who know a lot about technology get good **jobs** at renowned companies.

For me, being successful depends on the things you know how to do well. If you know how to do your job well, you always have opportunities to move up. Companies recognize the work of good employees by promoting them or extending their contract. Good employees always grow in their jobs when they show a good attitude. Therefore, a good attitude is also very important.

My great effort is to grow every day. I grow when I read interesting things. I grow when I exercise my skills and I grow when I do useful things with my time. If you want to grow, you

exitoso, debes crecer un **poquito** cada día más.

Si quieres ascender de puesto, si quieres crecer en los **negocios** o si quieres conocer más acerca de las destrezas útiles de la vida, debes leer muchos libros, artículos y revistas sobre las cosas que debes saber para tu trabajo y tu vida. Hoy tienes una buena oportunidad para crecer más. Si creces más hoy, creces **mañana**, y así, hasta ser una persona verdaderamente exitosa.

El éxito no es fácil, pero debes hacer el esfuerzo por ser una mejor persona.

must do this, too. If you waste your time on things that are not useful, you do not grow. To be successful, you must grow a little more each day.

If you want to move up, if you want to grow in **business** or if you want to know more about the useful life skills, you should read many books, articles and magazines about the things you should know for your work and your life. Today, you have a good opportunity to grow more. If you grow more today, you grow **tomorrow**, and so on, until you become a truly successful person.

Success is not easy, but you must make the effort to be a better person.

Por favor responda las siguientes preguntas.	Please answer the following questions.

¿Qué se necesita para ser exitoso?	What does it take to be successful?

_____

____

_____

____

_____

____

¿Cuál es una de las reglas de la vida?	What is one of the rules of life?

¿De qué está lleno la vida?	What is life full of?

_____

_____

_____

_____

¿Qué debemos conocer? | What should we know?

_____

_____

_____

_____

_____

_____

¿Qué pasa si no sabes de tecnología? | What happens if you do not know about technology?

_____

_____

_____

_____

_____

_____

¿De qué depende ser exitoso? | What does being successful depend on?

_____

_____

_____
___

_____
___

¿Qué pasa si sabes hacer bien tu trabajo?

What happens if you know how to do your job well?

_____
___

_____
___

_____
___

_____
___

_____
___

_____
___

¿Cuál es mi gran esfuerzo de todos los días?

What is my great effort every day?

_____
___

_____
___

_____
___

_____
___

_____
___

_____
___

_____
___

_____
___

¿Cuándo crezco?

When do I grow?

_____
___

_____
___

_____
___

_____
___

¿Qué debes hacer si quieres ascender de puesto?

What should you do if you want to move up?

_____
___

_____
___

_____
___

_____
___

Respuestas sugeridas	Suggested answers
¿Qué se necesita para ser exitoso?	What does it take to be successful?
Se necesita aprender muchas cosas útiles e importantes.	You need to learn many useful and important things.
¿Cuál es una de las reglas de la vida?	What is one of the rules of life?
Cuando una persona aprende lo necesario, siempre tiene oportunidad de éxito.	When a person learns what is necessary, they always have the chance to succeed.
¿De qué está lleno la vida?	What is life full of?
La vida está llena de cosas que debemos conocer.	Life is full of things we must know.
¿Qué debemos conocer?	What should we know?
Debemos conocer acerca de la tecnología y el internet.	We must know about technology and the internet.
¿Qué pasa si no sabes de tecnología?	What happens if you do not know about technology?
Es difícil obtener un buen empleo.	It is difficult to get a good job.

¿De qué depende ser exitoso?

What does being successful depend on?

Depende de las cosas que sabes hacer bien.

It depends on the things you know how to do well.

¿Qué pasa si sabes hacer bien tu trabajo?

What happens if you know how to do your job well?

Tienes oportunidades de ascender de puesto o extender tu contrato.

You have opportunities to promote or extend your contract.

¿Cuál es mi gran esfuerzo de todos los días?

What is my great effort every day?

Crecer es mi gran esfuerzo de todos los días.

Growing is my great effort every day.

¿Cuándo crezco?

When do I grow?

Crezco cuando leo cosas interesantes y hago cosas útiles con mi tiempo.

I grow when I read interesting things and do useful things with my time.

¿Qué debes hacer si quieres ascender de puesto?

What should you do if you want to move up?

Debes conocer más acerca de las destrezas útiles de la vida y leer mucho.

You must know more about life's useful skills and read a lot.

Lesson 5:
Present Simple with "ER" verbs

Español	English
Mis mascotas	**My Pets**
Vocabulario importante:	**Important vocabulary:**
cobaya	gerbil
conejillos de indias	guinea pig
gusto	taste
honestamente	honestly
mascota	pet
merecemos	deserve
roedores	rodents
ruido	noise
tiernos	sweet

varias	several

Tener una **mascota** es una experiencia singular. Todos **merecemos** tener un compañero especial en nuestras vidas. Para algunos, los perros son las mascotas ideales. Para otros, los gatos son los compañeros perfectos. También hay otras personas que tienen gusto por las aves, los peces o los reptiles. **Honestamente**, cualquier compañero es bueno cuando estás triste o melancólico.

Having a **pet** is a unique experience. We all **deserve** to have a special companion in our lives. For some, dogs are the ideal pets. For others, cats are the perfect companions. There are also other people who like birds, fish or reptiles. **Honestly**, any partner is good when you're sad or melancholy.

Para mí, las mascotas perfectas son los **roedores**. Animalitos como los hámster, ratones o **conejillos de indias** son mascotas idóneas. Éstos son animalitos que siempre están contigo y no hacen mucho **ruido**. Estos animalitos tampoco hacen desorden en tu casa. Los puedes tener en una jaula. Ellos son felices en su jaula con su comida.

For me, the perfect pets are **rodents**. Animals such as hamsters, mice or guinea pigs are ideal pets. These are animals that are always with you and do not make much **noise**. These little animals do not mess up your house either. You can have them in a cage. They are happy in their cage with their food.

Hay algunas personas que no tienen gusto por este tipo de mascota. Los entiendo. Entiendo a las personas que tienen **gusto** por los perros. Ellos corren en el parque con su perro o pueden hacer muchas más cosas. Pero estas personas no entienden porque mis mascotas favoritas

There are some people who do not like this type of pet. I understand them. I understand the people who have a **taste** for dogs. They run in the park with their dog or they can do many other things. But these people

son los roedores. Quizá no nos entendemos porque somos tan distintos.

Debo reconocer que tengo **varias** mascotas. Tengo un hámster, dos conejillos de indias, y varios ratones blancos. Reconozco que los ratones blancos son mascotas exóticas. Pero si tienes al menos uno, es seguro que te haces fan de inmediato. Para mí, los ratones blancos son tan lindos y **tiernos**. Son animalitos tan fáciles de querer.

Ahora, tengo otro problema: quiero una mascota nueva. Seguro, no quiero un perro. Los perros son lindos, pero no quiero uno. Quiero una mascota como una cobaya. Entiendo que no son comunes, pero son animalitos tan lindos y hermosos. Creo que son una buena adición a mi familia. Tengo bastante espacio en mi casa. Creo que no es difícil obtener al nuevo miembro de mi familia. ¡No puedo creer que pronto puedo tener a mi nueva cobaya!

do not understand why my favorite pets are rodents. Maybe we do not understand each other because we are so different.

I must admit that I have **several** pets. I have a hamster, two guinea pigs, and several white mice. I recognize that white mice are exotic pets. But if you have at least one, it's sure that you become a fan immediately. For me, white mice are so cute and sweet. They are animals so easy to love.

Now, I have another problem: I want a new pet. Sure, I do not want a dog. Dogs are cute, but I do not want one. I want a pet like a gerbil. I understand that they are not common, but they are cute and beautiful animals. I think they are a good addition to my family. I have enough space in my house. I think it's not difficult to get the new member of my family. I cannot believe that soon I can have my new gerbil!

Por favor responda las siguientes preguntas.

Please answer the following questions.

¿Cómo es la experiencia de tener una mascota?

What is the experience of having a pet like?

_____
___

_____
___

_____
___

_____
___

Para algunos, ¿Cuáles son las mascotas ideales?

To some, what are the ideal pets?

_____
___

_____
___

_____
___

_____
___

Para mí, ¿Cuáles son las mascotas ideales?

For me, what are the ideal pets?

_____
___

_____
___

_____
___

_____
___

___

_____
___

_____
___

¿Por qué son los roedores las mascotas ideales?

Why are rodents the ideal pets?

_____
___

_____
___

_____
___

_____
___

_____
___

_____
___

¿Dónde son felices estos animalitos?

Where are these little animals happy?

_____
___

_____
___

_____
___

_____
___

_____
___

_____
___

_____
___

_____
___

¿Por qué tienen gusto las personas por los perros?

Why do people like dogs?

_____
___

_____
___

_____
___

_____
___

¿Por qué no nos entendemos con estas personas?

Why do we not get along with these people?

_____
___

_____
___

_____
___

_____
___

¿Qué debo reconocer?

What should I admit?

_____
___

_____
___

_____
___

_____
——

¿Qué problema tengo?

_____
——
_____
——
_____
——

¿Cómo son las cobayas?

_____
——
_____
——
_____
——

_____
——

What problem do I have?

_____
——
_____
——
_____
——

What are gerbils like?

_____
——
_____
——
_____
——

Respuestas sugeridas	Suggested answers
¿Cómo es la experiencia de tener una mascota?	What is the experience of having a pet like?
<u>Es una experiencia singular.</u>	
	<u>It is a unique experience.</u>
Para algunos, ¿Cuáles son las mascotas ideales?	To some, what are the ideal pets?
<u>Para algunos, los perros son las mascotas ideales.</u>	
	<u>To some, dogs are the ideal pets.</u>
Para mí, ¿Cuáles son las mascotas ideales?	For me, what are the ideal pets?
	<u>For me, rodents are the ideal pets.</u>
<u>Para mí, los roedores son las mascotas ideales.</u>	
¿Por qué son los roedores las mascotas ideales?	Why are rodents the ideal pets?
<u>Siempre están contigo y no hacen mucho ruido.</u>	<u>They are always with you and they do not make much noise.</u>
¿Dónde son felices estos animalitos?	Where are these little animals happy?
<u>Son felices en su jaula con su</u>	<u>They are happy in their cage</u>

comida.	with their food.
¿Por qué tienen gusto las personas por los perros?	Why do people like dogs?
Los perros corren en el parque o pueden hacer muchas cosas.	Dogs run in the park or can do many things.
¿Por qué no nos entendemos con estas personas?	Why do we not get along with these people?
Porque somos muy distintos.	Because we are very different.
¿Qué debo reconocer?	What should I admit?
Debo reconocer que tengo varias mascotas.	I must admit that I have several pets.
¿Qué problema tengo?	What problem do I have?
Quiero una mascota nueva.	I want a new pet.
¿Cómo son las cobayas?	What are gerbils like?
Son animalitos lindos y tiernos.	They are cute and sweet animals.

SECTION IV

THE PRESENT CONTINUOUS TENSE

Lesson 6:
Present Continuous Tense

Español	English
La nueva casa	**The New House**
Vocabulario importante:	**Important vocabulary:**
aventuras	adventures
camión	truck
cargando	loading

casa de sueños	dream house
despidiendo	saying goodbye
frágiles	fragile
guardando	keeping
muchachos	guys
mudando	moving
peleas	fights

Hoy es un día super especial. Nos estamos **mudando** a nuestra nueva casa. Es una casa muy grande. Tiene cuatro habitaciones, tres baños, cocina, sala familiar, un garaje y un patio trasero enorme. Es una casa tan linda. Parece una **casa de sueños**.

Today is a super special day. We are **moving** to our new house. It's a very large house. It has four bedrooms, three bathrooms, kitchen, family room, a garage and a huge backyard. It's such a beautiful house. It looks like a **dream house**.

Mi padre está hablando con los **muchachos** del **camión**. Ellos deben llevarse todas nuestras cosas. La casa vieja está vacía. Solo hay cajas y nuestros muebles. Mi madre está revisando las últimas cosas. No se pueden perder nuestras cosas. Ella se está asegurando que todo está bien.

My father is talking to the **guys** in the **truck**. They must take all our things. The old house is empty. There are only boxes and our furniture. My mother is checking the last things. None of our things can get lost. She is making sure everything is fine.

Mis hermanos y yo estamos jugando por última vez en nuestro patio trasero. Tenemos muchas historias de nuestros juegos y nuestras **peleas**.

My brothers and I are playing for the last time in our backyard. We have many stories of our

Estamos recordando los juegos de nuestra casa. Ahora, estamos emocionados porque tenemos más espacio para nuestros juegos. Creo que tenemos espacio para nuevas **aventuras**. Nos gusta mucho el fútbol. Creo que tenemos suficiente espacio para jugar al fútbol en nuestra nueva casa.

games and our **fights**. We are remembering the games in our house. Now, we are excited because we have more space for our games. I think we have room for new **adventures**. We like soccer a lot. I think we have enough space to play soccer in our new home.

Los muchachos están **cargando** las cosas al camión. Están subiendo lo más pesado primero. Luego, van todas las cajas. Por último, van las cosas **frágiles**, es decir, las cosas que se quiebran. Mi madre está supervisando el trabajo de los muchachos.

The guys are **loading** things to the truck. They are loading up the heaviest first. Then, all the boxes go. Finally, the **fragile** things, that is, things that break, are loaded. My mother is supervising the work of the boys.

Mi padre está **guardando** algunas cosas en el auto. Él se lleva algunas cosas especiales como los álbumes de fotos, espejos y figuritas de cristal. Estas son cosas que se pueden arruinar en el camión grande. Siento que ya extraño esta casa. Hay muchos recuerdos de mi familia. Pero estoy feliz porque la nueva casa es bonita. Tiene todo lo que queremos.

My father is **keeping** some things in the car. He is taking some special things like photo albums, mirrors and crystal figurines. These are things that can be ruined in the big truck. I feel like I already miss this house. There are many memories of my family. But I'm happy because the new house is beautiful. It has everything we want.

Ya nos estamos **despidiendo** de la casa vieja. Adiós casa. Gracias

73

por tan lindos momentos. Tu nueva familia viene pronto. El camión se está marchando y nosotros estamos siguiéndole. Ya falta poco para estar en nuestra nueva casa. ¡No puede esperar más!

We are already **saying goodbye** to the old house. Goodbye house. Thanks for such nice moments. Your new family is coming soon. The truck is leaving, and we are following him. It's almost time to be in our new house. He cannot wait anymore!

Por favor responda las siguientes preguntas.

Please answer the following questions.

¿Por qué es hoy un día super especial?

Why is today a super special day?

_____

___

_____

___

_____

___

_____

___

¿Cómo es la nueva casa?

What is the new house like?

_____

___

_____

___

_____

___

_____

___

¿Con quién está hablando mi padre?

Who is my father talking to?

_____

___

_____

___

_____

___

———

——————

———

¿Qué está revisando mi madre? | What is my mother checking?

——————

———

——————

———

——————

———

¿Qué estamos haciendo por última vez? | What are we doing for the last time?

——————

———

——————

———

——————

———

¿Para qué tenemos espacio en la nueva casa? | What do we have space in the new house for?

——————

———

——————

———

_____	_____
___	___
_____	_____
___	___

¿Cuáles cosas van de último?	What things go last?
_____	_____
___	___
_____	_____
___	___
_____	_____
___	___

¿Qué cosas lleva mi padre en el auto?	What is my father taking in the car?
_____	_____
___	___
_____	_____
___	___
_____	_____
___	___
_____	_____
___	___

Respuestas sugeridas	Suggested answers
¿Por qué es hoy un día super especial?	Why is today a super special day?
Hoy es un día super especial porque nos estamos mudando de casa.	Today is a super special day because we are moving to a new house.
¿Cómo es la nueva casa?	What is the new house like?
Parece una casa de sueños.	It seems like a dream house.
¿Con quién está hablando mi padre?	Who is my father talking to?
Mi padre está hablando con los muchachos del camión.	My father is talking to the guys from the truck.
¿Qué está revisando mi madre?	What is my mother checking?
Mi madre está revisando las últimas cosas.	My mother is checking the last things.
¿Qué estamos haciendo por última vez?	What are we doing for the last time?
Mis hermanos y yo estamos jugando por última vez en nuestro patio trasero.	My brothers and I are playing for the last time in our backyard.

¿Para qué tenemos espacio en la nueva casa?	What do we have space in the new house for?
Creo que tenemos espacio para nuevas aventuras.	I think we have space for new adventures.
¿Cuáles cosas van de último?	What things go last?
Por último, van las cosas frágiles, es decir, las cosas que se quiebran.	Lastly, fragile things, that is, the things that break.
¿Qué cosas lleva mi padre en el auto?	What is my father taking in the car?
Mi padre lleva algunas cosas especiales como los álbumes de fotos, espejos y figuritas de cristal.	My father is taking some special things like photo albums, mirrors and crystal figurines.

SECTION V

THE PRESENT SIMPLE: IRREGULAR VERBS

Lesson 7:
Present Simple Tense: Irregular Verbs

Español	English
Obras de caridad	Charities

Vocabulario importante:	Important vocabulary:
aprecian	appreciate
contribución	contribution
corazón	heart
correcto	right
esperar	expect
medio ambiente	environment
miles	thousands
obras de caridad	charity

En mi familia, siempre damos lo que podemos a las **obras de caridad**. Apoyamos a las obras para la protección de los animales, el **medio ambiente** y la educación. Es una costumbre en mi familia contribuir a las buenas obras.

In my family, we always give what we can to **charity**. We support the organizations for the protection of animals, the **environment** and education. It is a custom in my family to contribute to good deeds.

Mi padre dice:

- Si tú no puedes hacer las cosas tú mismo, entonces da a las personas que sí lo hacen.

My father says:

- If you cannot do things yourself, then give to the people who do.

Por eso doy lo que puedo a las obras de caridad. Algunas veces no doy dinero. En algunas ocasiones doy ropa, zapatos, o comida. En realidad, muchas obras de caridad no piden dinero. Simplemente piden apoyo de personas de buen **corazón**. Cuando das de buen corazón, las personas **aprecian** tu ayuda grandemente.

That's why I give what I can to the charities. Sometimes I do not give money. Sometimes I give clothes, shoes, or food. Actually, many charities do not ask for money. They simply ask for support from people with a good heart. When you give from the heart, people **appreciate** your help greatly.

Sin embargo, existen personas que no dan a las obras de caridad. Está bien; pueden hacer lo que consideren **correcto**. Pero, estas personas no están pensando que existen otras personas que están haciendo mucho bien para nuestro mundo. Las personas que están trabajando para mejorar el mundo necesitan nuestro apoyo. Si no se lo damos, ¿qué podemos **esperar**?

However, there are people who do not give to charity. It's okay; they can do what they think is **right**. But, these people are not thinking that there are other people who are doing a lot of good for our world. The people who are working to improve the world need our support. If we do not give it to them, what can we **expect**?

81

No estoy diciendo que debes dar dinero. Pero sí puedes hacer algo. Si das tu tiempo, por ejemplo, apoyando alguna causa que en la que crees, están haciendo un cambio. Si das cosas ya no necesitas, hay **miles** de personas en el mundo que lo aprecian.

I'm not saying you should give money. But you can do something. If you give your time, for example, supporting a cause that you believe in, you are making a change. If you donate things you no longer need, there are **thousands** of people in the world who appreciate it.

Si das lo mejor de ti, le están dando al mundo una **contribución** maravillosa. Puedes hacer la diferencia con tus talentos y tu actitud. Si das lo mejor de ti siempre, los demás dan lo mejor de ellos. Es una cadena. Con esta actitud, te puedes asegurar que todos estamos dando lo mejor. Si damos lo mejor todos los días, el mundo cambia. Todos queremos el cambio. El cambio empieza con dar a los demás. No esperes que los demás te den. Empieza tú por dar a los demás.

If you give your best, you are giving the world a wonderful **contribution**. You can make a difference with your talents and your attitude. If you give your best always, others give their best. It is a chain. With this attitude, you can be sure that we are all giving our best. If we give our best every day, the world changes. We all want the change. The change begins with giving to others. Do not expect others to give you. Start by giving to others.

Por favor responda las siguientes preguntas.	Please answer the following questions.

¿Qué damos a las obras de caridad?

_____

___

_____

___

_____

___

_____

___

What do we give to charity?

_____

___

_____

___

_____

___

_____

___

¿Qué obras apoyamos?

_____

___

_____

___

_____

___

_____

___

What charities do we support?

_____

___

_____

___

_____

___

_____

___

¿Qué doy algunas veces a las obras de caridad?

_____

___

_____

___

_____

What do I sometimes give to charities?

_____

___

_____

___

——

—————————————

——

¿Qué piden las organizaciones?

—————————————

——

—————————————

——

—————————————

——

¿Qué necesitan las personas que están trabajando para mejorar el mundo?

—————————————

——

—————————————

——

—————————————

——

—————————————

——

——

—————————————

——

—————————————

——

What do organizations ask for?

—————————————

——

—————————————

——

—————————————

——

What do people who are working to improve the world need?

—————————————

——

—————————————

——

—————————————

——

¿Qué puedes dar a las obras de caridad si no es dinero?

What can you give charity if it's not money?

_____

___

_____

___

_____

___

_____

___

¿Cómo puedes hacer una contribución al mundo?

How can you make a contribution to the world?

_____

___

_____

___

_____

___

_____

___

¿Cómo te puedes asegurar de dar lo mejor?

How can you make sure to give the best?

_____

___

_____

___

_____

___

Respuestas sugeridas	Suggested answers
¿Qué damos a las obras de caridad?	What do we give to charity?
Damos lo que podemos a las obras de caridad.	We give what we can to charity.
¿Qué obras apoyamos?	What charities do we support?
Apoyamos a las obras para la protección de los animales, medio ambiente y la educación.	We support charities for the protection of animals, the environment and education.
¿Qué doy algunas veces a las obras de caridad?	What do I sometimes give to charities?
Algunas veces doy ropa, zapatos o comida.	I sometimes give clothes, shoes and food.
¿Qué piden las organizaciones?	What do organizations ask for?
Piden apoyo de personas con buen corazón.	Organizations ask for support from good-hearted people.
¿Qué necesitan las personas que están trabajando para mejorar el mundo?	What do people who are working to improve the world need?

<u>Nuestro apoyo.</u>	<u>Our support.</u>
¿Qué puedes dar a las obras de caridad si no es dinero?	What can you give charity if it's not money?
<u>Puedes dar tu tiempo.</u>	<u>You can give your time.</u>
¿Cómo puedes hacer una contribución al mundo?	How can you make a contribution to the world?
<u>Dando le mejor de ti.</u>	<u>The best of you.</u>
¿Cómo te puedes asegurar de dar lo mejor?	How can you make sure to give the best?
<u>Con una actitud de dar siempre lo mejor.</u>	<u>With the attitude of always giving your best.</u>

Lesson 8:
Present Simple Tense: Irregular Verbs

Español	English
Percepción	Perception

Vocabulario importante:	Important vocabulary:
atención	attention
común	common
comúnmente	commonly
frase	phrase
habilidad	ability
escuchar	listen
malentendidos	misunderstandings
percibir	perceive
repetir	repeat

sonido

Muchas personas me preguntan:

- ¿Cuál es la diferencia entre oír y escuchar?

Por ejemplo, "oigo la radio", pero "escucho música".

Esta es una pregunta muy **común**. Es una confusión normal cuando estás aprendiendo español. De hecho, es perfectamente usual que las personas nativo-parlantes del español también tienen esta duda acerca de estas palabras.

La diferencia se basa en la **atención** de las personas que hacen la actividad.

Por ejemplo, cuando "oyes la radio" estás hablando de la **habilidad** que tienes de oír, es decir, percibir sonido. Si no puedes oír, entonces, no puedes **percibir** sonido. Cuando una persona no puede oír, se dice que esta persona es "sorda". Entonces, "sorda" o "sordo" quiere decir que la persona no tiene la habilidad de oír.

sound

Many people ask me:

- What is the difference between hearing and listening?

For example, "I hear the radio," but "I listen to music."

This is a very **common** question. It is a normal confusion when you are learning Spanish. In fact, it is quite usual for native speakers of Spanish to have this doubt about these words as well.

The difference is based on the **attention** of the people who do the activity.

For example, when you "hear the radio" you are talking about your **ability** to hear, that is, to perceive sound. If you cannot hear, then you cannot **perceive** sound. When a person cannot hear, it is said that this person is "deaf." So, "deaf" means that the person does not have the ability to hear.

Ahora bien, cuando escuchas música, estás oyendo la música porque tienes la habilidad de percibir el **sonido**. La diferencia es que, si estás poniendo atención a la música, entonces estás escuchando. Esa es la diferencia. También hay muchas otras cosas que puedes **escuchar**. Puedes escuchar una charla, una conferencia, a otra persona hablar o a los pajaritos por la mañana.

Una frase **comúnmente** utilizada es "no oigo". Esta frase se utiliza cuando no puedes percibir sonido. Por ejemplo, estás hablando por teléfono y no se oye el audio. Cuando oyes, entonces puedes decir "te escucho" a la otra persona. Esto indica que sí oyes bien.

Durante una conversación le puedes decir a la otra persona:

- "perdón, ¿puedes **repetir**?"

Puedes usar esta **frase** cuando no oyes algo, o bien, no entiendes claramente. Esto es importante ya que algunas veces oímos algo distinto de lo que la persona está diciendo. Por eso es necesario aclarar bien las conversaciones.

Now, when you listen to music, you are hearing music because you have the ability to perceive **sound**. The difference is that, if you are paying attention to the music, then you are listening. That is the difference. There are also many other things that you can listen to. You can **listen** to a talk, a conference, to another person to talk or to the birds in the morning.

A **commonly** used phrase is "I do not hear". This phrase is used when you cannot perceive sound. For example, you are talking on the phone and you cannot hear the audio. When you hear, then you can say "I hear you" to the other person. This indicates that you do hear well.

During a conversation you can tell the other person:

- "Excuse me, can you repeat?"

You can use this **phrase** when you do not hear something, or, you do not understand clearly. This is important because sometimes we hear something

Así, evitamos **malentendidos** durante una conversación. Así, siempre estamos en la misma página.

other than what the person is saying. That is why it is necessary to clarify the conversations well. Thus, we avoid misunderstandings during a conversation. Thus, we are always on the same page.

Por favor responda las siguientes preguntas.

Please answer the following questions.

¿Cuál es una confusión normal cuando estás aprendiendo español?

What is a normal confusion when you are learning Spanish?

_____

_____

_____

¿En qué se basa la diferencia?

What is the difference based on?

_____

_____

_____

¿Qué haces cuando oyes?

What do you do when you hear?

_____

_____

_____

_____

_____

_____

¿Qué pasa cuando pones atención a la música?

What happens when you pay attention to the music?

_____

_____

_____

_____

_____

_____

_____

_____

_____

_____

_____

_____

¿Cuál es una frase comúnmente utilizada?

What is a commonly used phrase?

_____

_____

_____

_____

_____

_____

_____

_____

_____

_____

_____

_____

¿Qué frase puedes usar durante una conversación?

What phrase can you use during conversation?

_____   _____
——   ——

_____   _____
——   ——

_____   _____
——   ——

_____   _____
——   ——

¿Cuándo puedes usar esta frase?   When can you use this phrase?

_____   _____
——   ——

_____   _____
——   ——

_____   _____
——   ——

_____   _____
——   ——

¿Cómo se puede evitar malentendidos?   How can you avoid misunderstandings?

_____   _____
——   ——

_____   _____
——   ——

_____   _____
——   ——

_____   _____
——   ——

Respuestas sugeridas	Suggested answers
¿Cuál es una confusión normal cuando estás aprendiendo español?	What is a normal confusion when you are learning Spanish?
<u>La diferencia entre oír y escuchar es una confusión normal cuando estás aprendiendo español.</u>	<u>The difference between hear and listen is a common confusion when you are learning Spanish.</u>
¿En qué se basa la diferencia?	What is the difference based on?
<u>La diferencia se basa en la atención.</u>	<u>The difference is based on attention.</u>
¿Qué haces cuando oyes?	What do you do when you hear?
<u>Percibes sonido.</u>	<u>You perceive sound.</u>
¿Qué pasa cuando pones atención a la música?	What happens when you pay attention to the music?
<u>Estas escuchando la música.</u>	<u>You are listening to music.</u>
¿Cuál es una frase comúnmente utilizada?	What is a commonly used phrase?
<u>"No oigo" es una clase comúnmente utilizada.</u>	<u>"I can't hear" is a commonly used phrase.</u>

¿Qué frase puedes usar durante una conversación?	What phrase can you use during conversation?
Perdón, puedes repetir.	Sorry, can you repeat?
¿Cuándo puedes usar esta frase?	When can you use this phrase?
La puedes usar cuando no oyes bien.	You can use it when you don't hear well.
¿Cómo se puede evitar malentendidos?	How can you avoid misunderstandings?
Aclarar bien las conversaciones evita malentendidos.	You can avoid misunderstandings by clearing things up.

Lesson 9:
Present Simple Tense: Irregular Verbs

Español	English
Compras en línea	**Online Shopping**

Vocabulario importante:	**Important vocabulary:**
aplicación	application
compras en línea	online shopping
electrónicos	electronics
entrega	delivery
gigantesca	gigantic
hoy en día	nowadays
ítems	items
pedimos	order
posteo	posting
teléfonos móviles	mobile phone

Las **compras en línea** son muy populares **hoy en día**. Existen plataformas como Amazon e eBay. Estas plataformas permiten que las personas pidan artículos en línea. Revisan el **posteo** del artículo y luego lo piden. Se paga por el artículo por medio de una tarjeta de crédito o por algún otro medio electrónico.

Los **ítems** que se pueden comprar en línea son numerosos.

Online shopping is very popular **nowadays**. There are platforms like Amazon and eBay. These platforms allow people to order items online. They review the **posting** of the item and then they ask for it. You pay for the item by means of a credit card or by some other electronic means.

Se puede comprar ropa, zapatos, **electrónicos**, libros, juguetes y muchos otros ítems más. Cuando pides algún artículo en línea, debes esperar el tiempo de **entrega**. Los pedidos llegan a la puerta de tu casa u oficina. Esto depende del medio de entrega. Si pides entrega *express*, tus ítems llegan en menos de dos días.

Mis amigos y yo hacemos muchas compras en línea. **Pedimos** diversos artículos como ropa, zapatos, video juegos y **teléfonos móviles**. Lo que no pedimos en línea es comida. Existen servicios que te llevan comida a tu casa por medio de una aplicación en tu teléfono, pero preferimos salir a un restaurante a comer. De igual manera, muchas personas piden comida desde la **aplicación** de su teléfono móvil.

Cuando pides un artículo en línea, tu pedido es administrado por una empresa como **gigantesca** Amazon, o bien, una empresa más pequeña, usualmente local. Luego, la empresa procesa tu pedido y despacha tu ítem lo más pronto posible.

The **items** that can be purchased online are numerous. You can buy clothes, shoes, **electronics**, books, toys and many other items. When you order an item online, you must wait for the **delivery** time. Orders arrive at the door of your home or office. This depends on the delivery medium. If you ask for express delivery, your items arrive in less than two days.

My friends and I do a lot of shopping online. We **order** various items such as clothes, shoes, video games and **mobile phones**. What we do not order online is food. There are services that bring food to your home through an application on your phone, but we prefer to go to a restaurant to eat. Nevertheless, many people ask for food from the application of their mobile phone.

When you order an item online, your order is managed by a **gigantic** Amazon company, or a smaller one, usually a local company. Then, the company processes your order and dispatches your item as soon as

Las compras en línea te permiten comprar directamente de los fabricantes en algunos casos. Esto supone que es más barato y rápido. Pero, si compras directamente de la fábrica en China, por ejemplo, los ítems pueden tardar mucho tiempo en llegar a tu casa.

Mi amiga, Alicia, cuando ella pide en línea, pide artículos que no necesita inmediatamente. Si se tarde semanas en llegar a su casa, no importa. No lo necesita inmediatamente. Por eso, si tú necesitas algo inmediatamente, es mejor pedir el artículo de un vendedor local, o bien, ir a la tienda a buscarlo tú mismo.

possible.

Online purchases allow you to buy directly from the manufacturers in some cases. This assumes that it is cheaper and faster. But, if you buy directly from the factory in China, for example, the items may take a long time to arrive at your home.

My friend, Alicia, when she orders online, she orders items she does not need immediately. If it takes weeks to get home, it does not matter; she does not need it immediately. Therefore, if you need something immediately, it is better to order the item from a local seller or go to the store to find it yourself.

Por favor responda las siguientes preguntas.

Please answer the following questions.

¿Qué es popular hoy en día?

What is popular nowadays?

_____

____

_____

____

_____

____

_____

____

¿Qué plataformas existen?

What platforms exist?

_____

____

_____

____

_____

____

_____

____

¿Cuántos ítems se pueden comprar en línea?

How many items can you buy online?

_____

____

_____

____

_____

____

_____

___

___

_____

___

¿Qué se puede comprar?

What can you buy?

_____

___

_____

___

_____

___

_____

___

_____

___

_____

___

_____

___

¿Qué debes esperar cuando compras un ítem en línea?

What to expect when you buy an item online?

_____

___

_____

___

_____

___

_____

___

_____

___

¿Qué pedimos con mis amigos?

What do we order with my friends?

_____

___

_____

___

_____

___

_____

_____

_____

¿Qué servicios existen para llevar comida a tu casa?

_____

What services exist to deliver food to your home?

_____

_____

_____

_____

_____

_____

_____

_____

_____

_____

_____

_____

_____

_____

_____

¿Qué pasa cuando pides un artículo en línea?

_____

What happens when you order and article online?

_____

_____

_____

_____

_____

_____

_____

_____

_____

_____

_____

_____

_____

_____

_____

Respuestas sugeridas	Suggested answers
¿Qué es popular hoy en día?	What is popular nowadays?
Las compras en línea son muy populares hoy en día.	Online shopping is very popular nowadays.
¿Qué plataformas existen?	What platforms exist?
Existen plataformas como Amazon e eBay.	There are platforms like Amazon and eBay.
¿Cuántos ítems se pueden comprar en línea?	How many items can you buy online?
Son numerosos los ítems que se pueden comprar en línea.	There are numerous items that you can purchase online.
¿Qué se puede comprar?	What can you buy?
Se puede comprar ropa, zapatos, electrónicos, libros, juguetes y muchos otros ítems más.	You can buy clothes, shoes, electronics, books, toys and many other items.
¿Qué debes esperar cuando compras un ítem en línea?	What to expect when you buy an item online?
Debes esperar el tiempo de entrega.	You must wait the delivery time

¿Qué pedimos con mis amigos?

What do we order with my friends?

Pedimos diversos artículos como ropa, zapatos, video juegos y teléfonos móviles.

We order several items such as clothes, shoes, video games and mobile phones.

¿Qué servicios existen para llevar comida a tu casa?

What services exist to deliver food to your home?

Existen servicios que te llevan comida a tu casa por medio de una aplicación en tu teléfono.

There are services that will take food to your home through an application on your phone.

¿Qué pasa cuando pides un artículo en línea?

What happens when you order and article online?

Cuando pides un artículo en línea, tu pedido es administrado por una empresa como gigantesca Amazon, o bien, una empresa más pequeña, usualmente local

When you order an article online, your order is managed by a gigantic company like Amazon, or a small company, usually local.

SECTION VI

BRINGING IT ALL TOGETHER

Lesson 10:
Bringing it all together

Español	English
La música es una pasión	Music is a Passion
Vocabulario importante:	**Important vocabulary:**
concierto	concert
discos	discs
famosos	famous
fuerte	strong

géneros	genres
melodía	melody
público	public
ritmo	rhythm
una vez	once
variedades	varieties
velocidad	speed

La música es una pasión para millones de personas en todo el mundo. La música viene en todo tipo de **variedades**. La música es tan distinta y variable como el ser humano. Los diferentes tipos de música se conocen como "**géneros**". Un género musical es un tipo de música particular según su **melodía**, **ritmo** y **velocidad**.

Music is a passion for millions of people around the world. Music comes in all kinds of **varieties**. Music is as different and varied as human beings. The different types of music are known as "**genres**". A musical genre is a particular type of music based on its **melody**, **rhythm** and **speed**.

Existen una gran cantidad de géneros musicales. Los más **famosos** son: rock, pop, clásica, baladas, salsa, y electrónica, entre tanto otro más. Además, la popularidad de los géneros musicales también es relativo a países y regiones particulares.

There are a lot of musical genres. The most **famous** are: rock, pop, classical, ballads, salsa, and electronics, among others. In addition, the popularity of musical genres is also relative to particular countries and regions.

Una de las actividades más populares en cualquier ciudad es un **concierto**. Un concierto consiste en una banda, cantante o agrupación que interpreta su

One of the most popular activities in any city is a **concert**. A concert consists of a band,

música para el **público**. En todas las ciudades grandes, siempre hay conciertos. Puedes revisar quienes están cantando en tu ciudad en este momento. También puedes ver quienes están por venir.

En mi ciudad, varias bandas de rock están tocando. Estos conciertos son emocionantes. La música es **fuerte**, pero la experiencia es única. También se están interpretando obras musicales. Éstas son obras de teatro, pero con música y canto. Son obras fabulosas. Debes ir al menos **una vez** en la vida.

Los boletos para los conciertos se están vendiendo en línea. Puedes ingresar al sitio web de los organizadores para comprar tus boletos. En definitiva, la tecnología está facilitando la compra de boletos para estos magníficos conciertos.

En la actualidad, también se están ofreciendo suscripciones a servicios de música digital. Cuando obtienes tu suscripción, puedes acceder a millones de canciones. Ya no tienes que comprar cientos de **discos**. Ahora, puedes acceder a toda tu

singer or group that performs its music for the **public**. In all the big cities, there are always concerts. You can check who is singing in your city right now. You can also see who is coming.

In my city, several rock bands are playing. These concerts are exciting. The music is **loud**, but the experience is unique. Musical shows are also performed. These are plays, but with music and singing. They are fabulous works. You must go at least **once** in your life.

Tickets for the concerts are being sold online. You can access the organizers' website to buy your tickets. In short, technology is facilitating the purchase of tickets for these magnificent concerts.

Currently, subscriptions to digital music services are also being offered. When you get your subscription, you can access millions of songs. You do not have to buy hundreds of

música favorita en una sola suscripción. Entonces, si estás en el tráfico, no importa, puedes acceder a toda tu música en un solo dispositivo.

discs anymore. Now, you can access all your favorite music in a single subscription. So, if you're in traffic, it does not matter, you can access all your music on a single device.

Por favor responda las siguientes preguntas.

¿Qué es la música?

_____
___
_____
___
_____
___

Please answer the following questions.

What is music?

_____
___
_____
___
_____
___

¿En qué tipos viene la música?

_____
___
_____
___
_____
___

What types of music are there?

_____
___
_____
___
_____
___

¿Cuáles son los géneros musicales?

_____
___
_____
___
_____
___

What are musical genres?

_____
___
_____
___
_____
___

¿Qué es un concierto?

_____
___

_____
___

_____
___

What is a concert?

_____
___

_____
___

_____
___

¿Cómo son los conciertos?

_____
___

_____
___

_____
___

_____
___

What are concerts like?

_____
___

_____
___

_____
___

_____
___

¿Dónde se venden los boletos de los conciertos?

_____
___

_____
___

_____
___

Where are tickets for concerts sold?

_____
___

_____
___

_____
___

Respuestas sugeridas	Suggested answers
¿Qué es la música?	What is music?
La música es una pasión para millones de personas.	Music is a passion for millions of people.
¿En qué tipos viene la música?	What types of music are there?
La música viene en todo tipo de variedades.	Music comes is all types of varieties.
¿Cuáles son los géneros musicales?	What are musical genres?
Los géneros más famosos son: rock, pop, clásica, baladas, salsa y electrónica.	The most famous genres are: rock, pop, classical, ballads, salsa and electronic.
¿Qué es un concierto?	What is a concert?
Un concierto consiste en una banda, cantante o agrupación que interpreta su música para el público.	A concert consists in a band, singer or group that plays their music for the public.
¿Cómo son los conciertos?	What are concerts like?
Los conciertos son emocionantes.	Concerts are exciting.

¿Dónde se venden los boletos de los conciertos?

Where are tickets for concerts sold?

Los boletos para los conciertos se están vendiendo en línea.

Tickets for concerts are being sold online.

CONCLUSION

Wow! It seems like we just got started and we are already at this point. It has certainly been an interesting trip. We hope that the contents and materials in this book have helped you to improve your overall Spanish skills. We are certain that you have put in your best effort in order to do so.

That is why our recommendation is to go back to any of the lessons which you feel you need to review and go over the content. Of course, the more you practice, the better your skills will be. Indeed, your overall skills will improve in so far as you continue to practice.

So, do take this opportunity to continue building on your current skills. You will find that over time, you will progressively gain more and more understanding of the language you encounter on a daily basis.

Given the fact that there are a number of resources out there which can help you to practice your listening skills, such as movies, *telenovelas* and music, you will be able to put this content into practice right away.

Thank you once again for choosing this book. We hope to have met your expectations. And please don't forget to leave a comment. Other folks who are interested in learning Spanish will certainly find your reviews on this book useful.

See you in the next level!

CPSIA information can be obtained
at www.ICGtesting.com
Printed in the USA
LVHW010837120121
676186LV00008B/227